Sarah Dilger

Ready, Set, Grow!

American English

Student's Book 3

with Digital Pack

CAMBRIDGE

Our Book

3

Hello Again!

🎧 01 Listen. 👄 Say. 🖍 Color.

go to the bathroom

read a book

play a game

go outside

have a snack

have a drink

Welcome **Vocabulary Presentation:** go outside, go to the bathroom, have a drink, have a snack, play a game, read a book

Extra
Count.

Listen. **Point.** **Say.**

Color.

Say. Match.

Extra

Mime.

1 Our Day

Listen. Point. Sing.

go to school

go home

get up

have breakfast

have lunch

have dinner

wash my hands

go to bed

Extra Circle.

Vocabulary Presentation and Song: get up, go home, go to bed, go to school, have breakfast, have dinner, have lunch, wash my hands

Unit 1 **7**

Say. Stick. Color.

Extra
Count.

Point. **Say.** **Circle.**

Count.

Language Presentation: I (get up). **Unit 1** 9

Listen. Point. Circle.

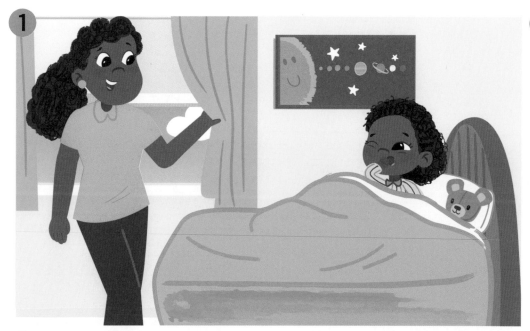

Extra
Circle.

 Look. Circle.

Extra
Color.

Watch. **Say.** **Match.**

brush my teeth

Extra
Check.

Look. **Check.** **Say.**

Think. ◯ Circle. ✏ Draw.

Extra
Trace.

2 Dinnertime

▶ 🎧 **Listen.** 🎵 **Sing.** 🖍 **Color.**

toast

jelly

meat

pizza

rice

fish

tomatoes

carrots

Say. Stick. Draw.

16 Unit 2 Vocabulary Practice

Extra
Count.

Point. Match. Say.

Circle.

Language Presentation: I have (fish) for (dinner). I don't have (rice) for (dinner).

Listen. **Point.** **Circle.**

1

2

3

4

Extra
Color.

5

6

 Draw. Say.

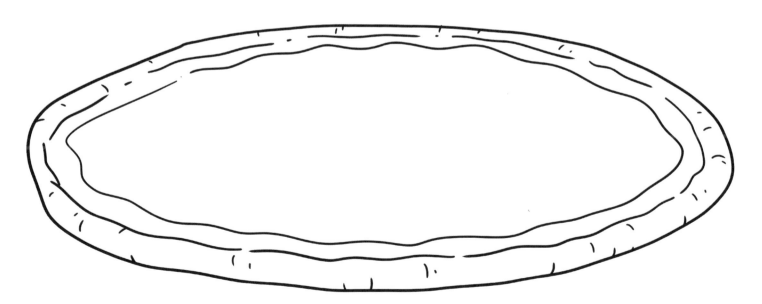

 Extra
Color.

Think. **Find.**  **Say.**

   eggs

vegetables

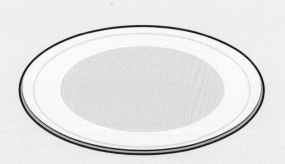

candy

chips

chocolate

Extra

Draw.

Circle. Draw. Say.

①

②

③

Color.

Look. **Think.** **Color.**

Well-being: I feel like I enjoy things.

Extra

Circle.

3 With My Friends

Listen. Sing. Circle.

build a fort

ride a scooter

watch a video

make a sandcastle

listen to music

ride a bike

dress up

dance

Extra
Count.

Say. **Stick.** **Color.**

Extra

Circle.

Listen. **Circle.** **Say.**

Listen. **Point.** **Circle.**

1

2

3

4

Extra
Color.

 Find. Check.

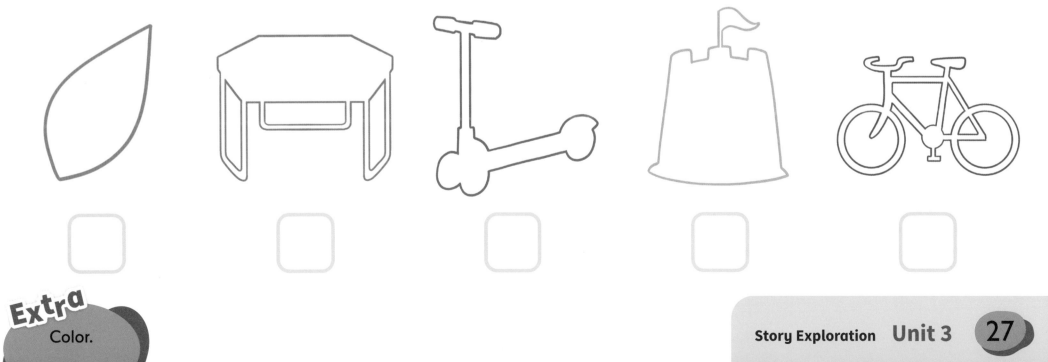

Extra
Color.

Watch. **Say.** **Match.**

cart

street

Extra

Count.

Look. Draw.

Unit 3 **Well-being:** I don't feel lonely.

Extra

Circle.

4 Our Faces

blond

short

nose

glasses

long

eyes

hair

mouth

Count.

Vocabulary Presentation and Song: eyes, glasses, hair, mouth, nose; blond, long, short **Unit 4** 31

Say. Stick. Color.

Extra
Circle.

Listen. **Color.**

(1) (2) (3) (4)

(1) (2) (3) (4)

(1) (2) (3) (4)

(1) (2) (3) (4)

Count.

Listen. **Point.** **Color.**

1

2

3

4

Extra
Find.

5

6

 Look.  Match.

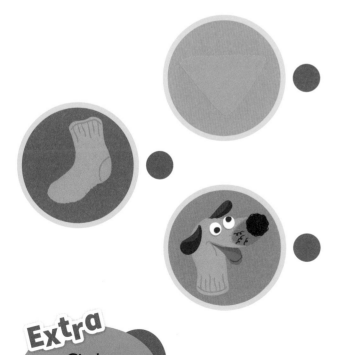

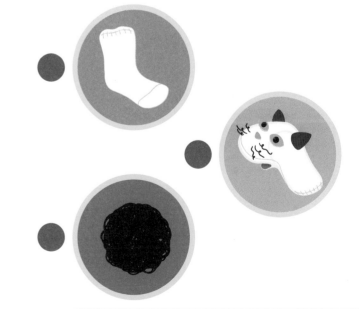

Extra

Circle.

Look. **Match.**

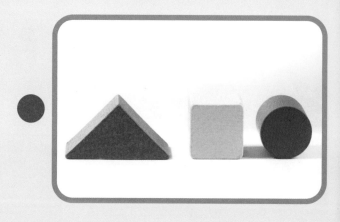

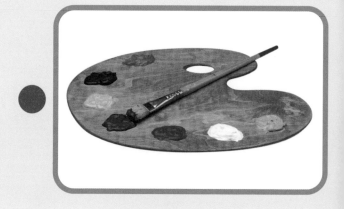

Extra
Circle.

Point. Draw. Say.

①

②

③

④

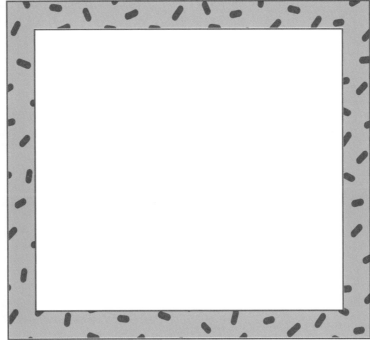

Circle.

Look. Draw.

me

hobby

like

love

Extra
Circle.

5 On the Farm

Listen. Sing. Circle.

goat

horse

cow

tail

chicken

beak

wings

duck

Extra
Count.

Vocabulary Presentation and Song: chicken, cow, duck, goat, horse; beak, tail, wings

Say. Stick. Color.

Extra
Circle.

Look. Match. Say.

Extra
Count.

Listen. **Point.** **Count.**

1

2

3

4

Extra
Circle.

5

6

 Count. Color.

Count.

Look. Match. Say.

farm

jungle

ocean

Extra

Color.

 Circle. Point. Say.

1

2

 Circle.

Color. **Say.** **Draw.**

Unit 5 **Well-being:** I feel like I'm excited.

Extra

Draw.

6 Clothes for Today

  Listen. Sing. Color.

shorts

sneakers

pants

boots

dress

T-shirt

skirt

sandals

Circle.

Say. Stick. Draw.

Extra

Count.

Check. **Listen.** **Say.**

Extra
Color.

Language Presentation: It's (hot) today. I'm wearing (sandals). I'm not wearing (boots). **Unit 6** 49

Listen. **Point.** **Circle.**

1

2

3

4

Extra
Circle.

5

6

 Look. ◯ Circle.

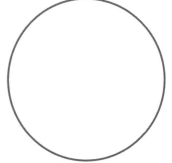

Extra

Draw.

Look. Match.

plant

give away

recycle

cotton

Extra
Circle.

Look. Match. Say.

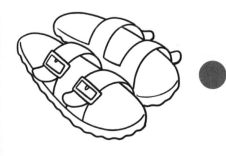

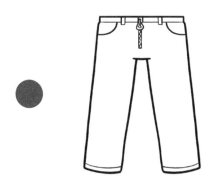

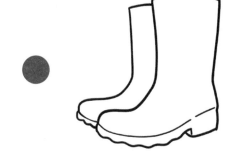

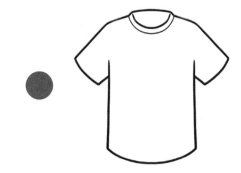

Color.

Review: It's (hot) today. I'm wearing (sandals). I'm not wearing (boots). **Unit 6** 53

Look. Draw.

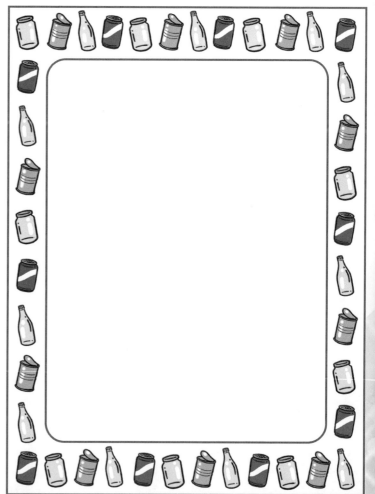

Well-being: I feel good when I recycle.

Extra

Color.

7 At School

Listen. Sing. Circle.

help

build a tower

paint a picture

do a puzzle

share

cut

make a toy

clean up

Extra Find.

Vocabulary Presentation and Song: build a tower, clean up, cut, do a puzzle, help, make a toy, paint a picture, share **Unit 7** 55

Say. Stick. Color.

Extra
Count.

Listen. Circle. Say.

①

②

③

④

Extra
Mime.

Language Presentation: He / She is (doing a puzzle).   Unit 7   57

Listen. **Point.** **Check.**

1

2

3

4

Extra
Color.

5

6

🔍 Find. ⭕ Circle.

2 4 6

1 2 6

1 3 5

2 4 6

Extra
Color.

Look. Match.

scissors

paper plate

●　　　　●　　　　●　　　　●　　　　●

Extra

Circle.

Find. Match. Say.

Extra
Circle.

Color . Draw.

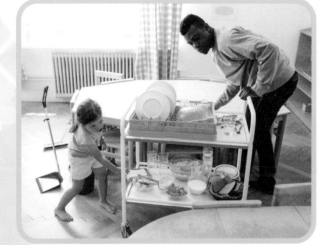

Unit 7 **Well-being:** I feel like I'm doing well (at school).

Extra
Color.

8 At the Party

Listen. Sing. Circle.

balloon

HAPPY BIRTHDAY

birthday party

candle

cake

family

card

present

costume

Extra

Color.

Say. Stick. Draw.

Extra
Count.

Find. **Circle.** **Say.**

Count.

Listen. **Point.** **Check.**

1

2

3

4

Extra

Circle.

5

6

 Find. Circle. 😃 Say.

Extra
Count.

Look. Match.

Thanksgiving

Lunar New Year

Carnival

dragon

Extra
Choose.

Find. **Match.** **Say.**

Draw. Say.

Extra
Color.

9 On the Playground

Listen. Sing. Circle.

tunnel

jungle gym

swing

bridge

slide

seesaw

sandbox

merry-go-round

Extra

Count.

Vocabulary Presentation and Song: bridge, jungle gym, merry-go-round, sandbox, seesaw, slide, swing, tunnel

Say. Stick. Color.

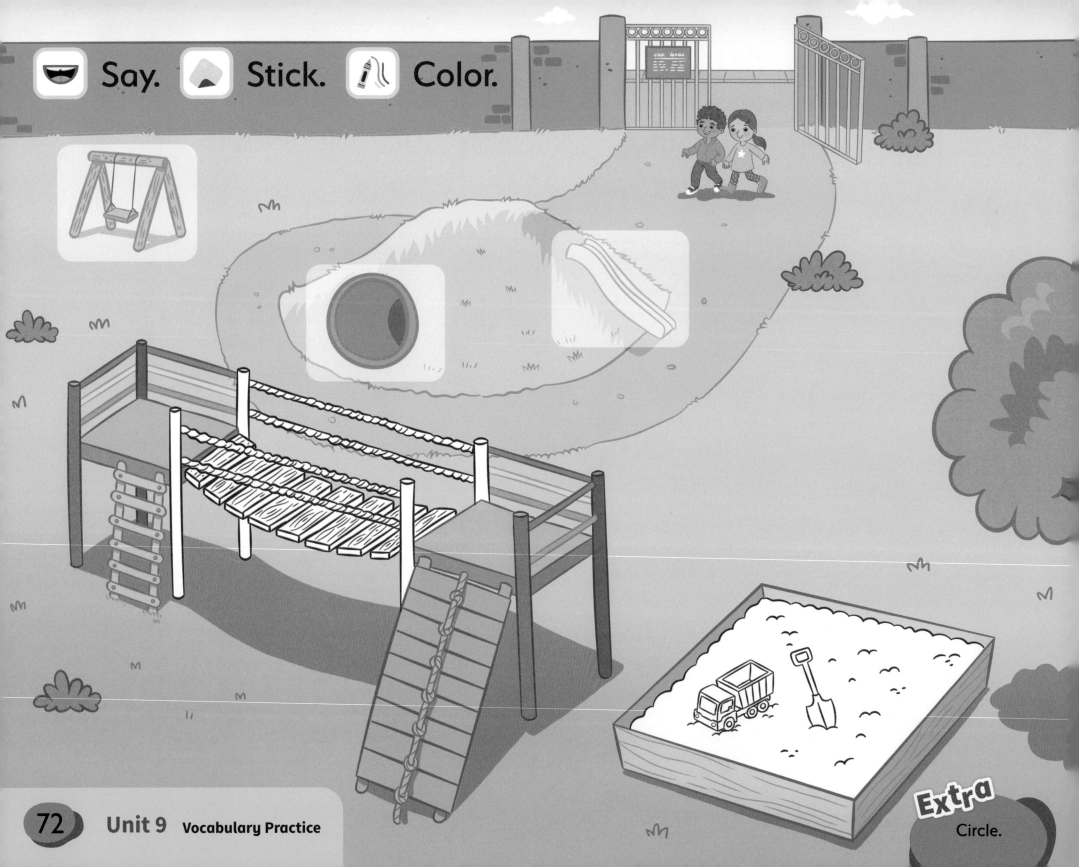

Extra

Circle.

Chant. **Match.** **Say.**

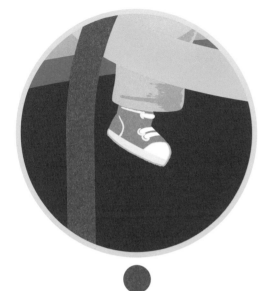   

Extra

Color.

Language Presentation: Where is (she)? Is (she) on the (bridge)? Yes, (she) is. / No, (she) isn't. **Unit 9** 73

Listen. Point. Circle.

1

2

3

4

Extra
Color.

5

6

 Find. Draw lines.

Circle.

Look. Match.

trampoline

crawl

monkey bars

climb

Extra

Circle.

🔍 **Find.** 🖍 **Color.** 😬 **Say.**

①

②

③

④

⑤

⑥

Extra
Count.

Review: Where is (she)? Is (she) on the (bridge)? Yes, (she) is. / No, (she) isn't. **Unit 9** 77

Look. ✔ Check. ✏ Draw.

Extra
Circle.

Trace. **Say.** **Circle.**

26

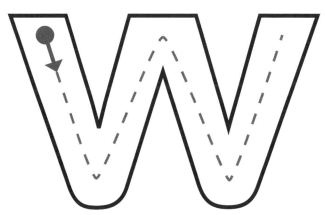

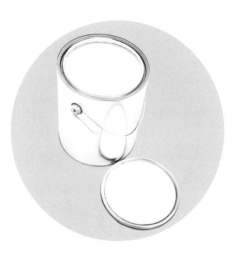

Color.

Trace. **Say.** **Circle.**

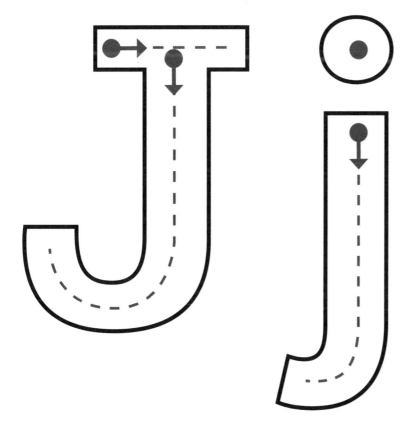

Extra
Color.

Trace. **Say.** **Circle.**

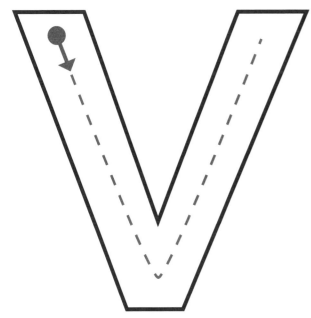 

Extra
Color.

Trace. **Say.** **Circle.**

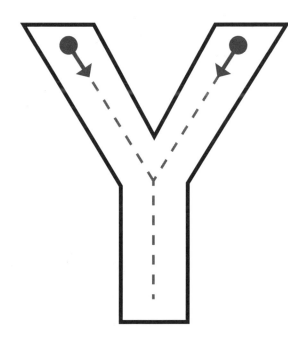

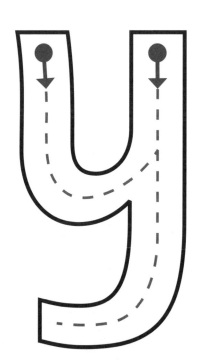

Extra
Color.

Trace. Say. Circle.

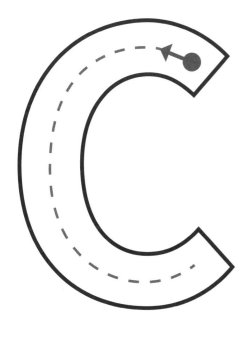
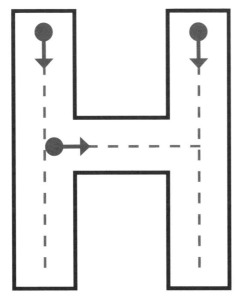
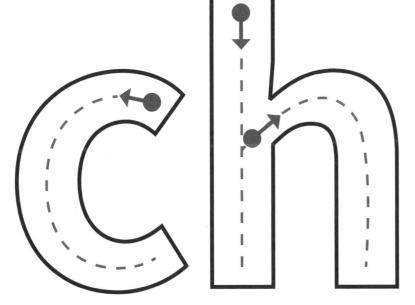

Extra
Color.

CH, ch **Sounds** 83

Trace. **Say.** **Circle.**

 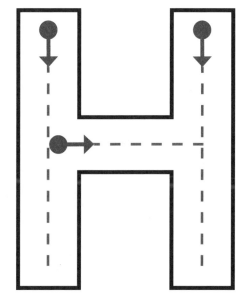

 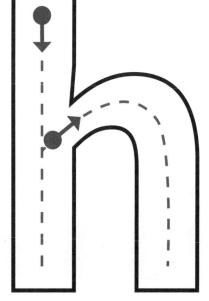

Extra
Color.

Trace. Say. Circle.

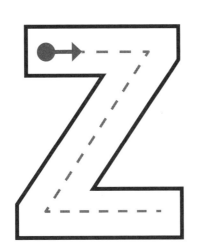

Extra
Color.

33 **Trace.** **Say.** **Circle.**

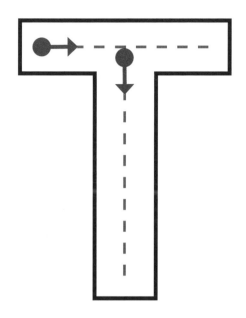 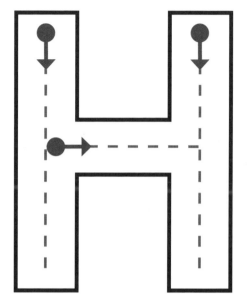

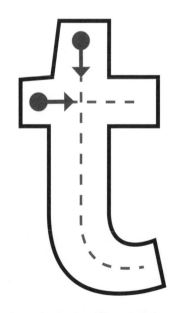 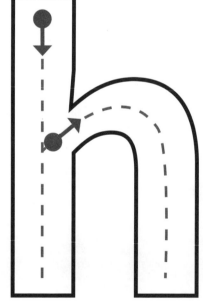

Extra
Color.

Trace. **Say.** **Circle.**

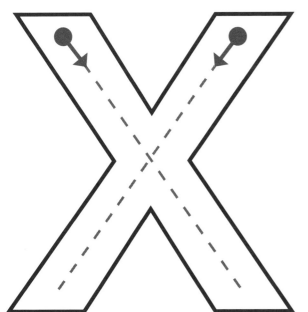

Color.

Count. Circle. Listen.

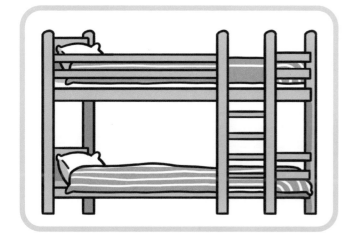

1 2 3 4

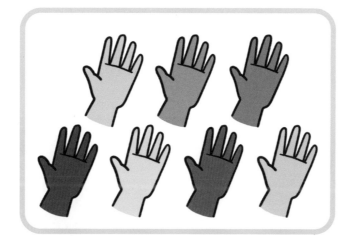

5 6 7 8

9 10 11 12

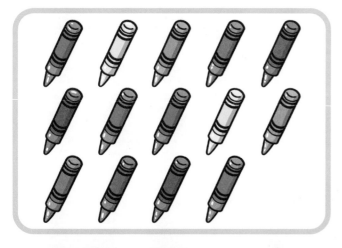

13 14 15

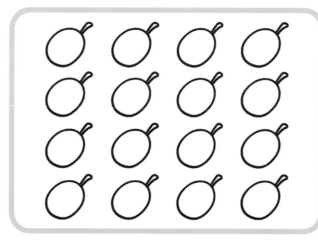

16 17 18

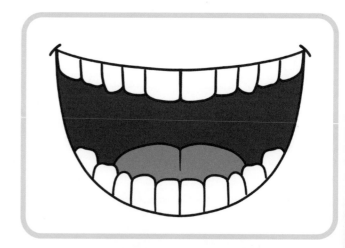

19 20

Extra
Color.

Chant. **Trace.** **Say.**

30 **40**

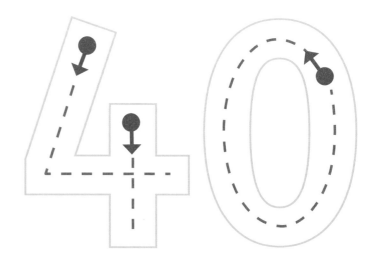

Chant. **Trace.** **Say.**

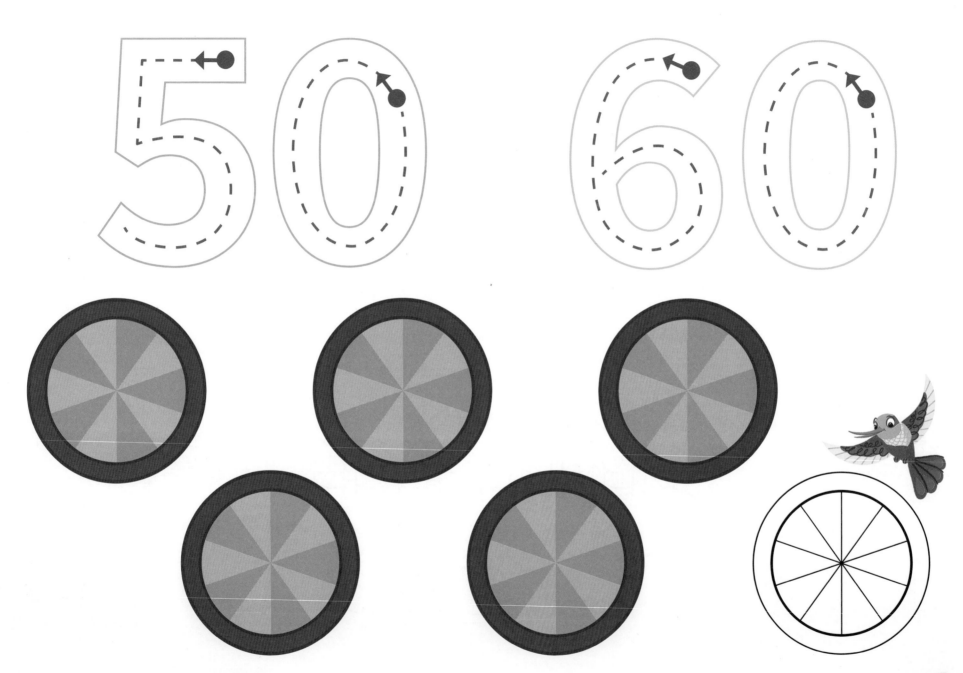

Extra
Color.

Chant. **Count.** **Color.**

10 20 30 40 50 60 / 20

10 50 / 20 30 40 50 60

10 20 30 / 40 40 50 60

10 20 30 20 / 40 50 60

Extra
Copy.

Extra
Color.

Chant. **Trace.** **Say.**

90 100

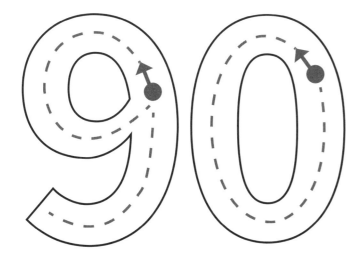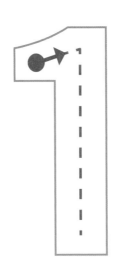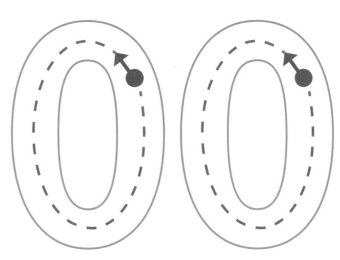

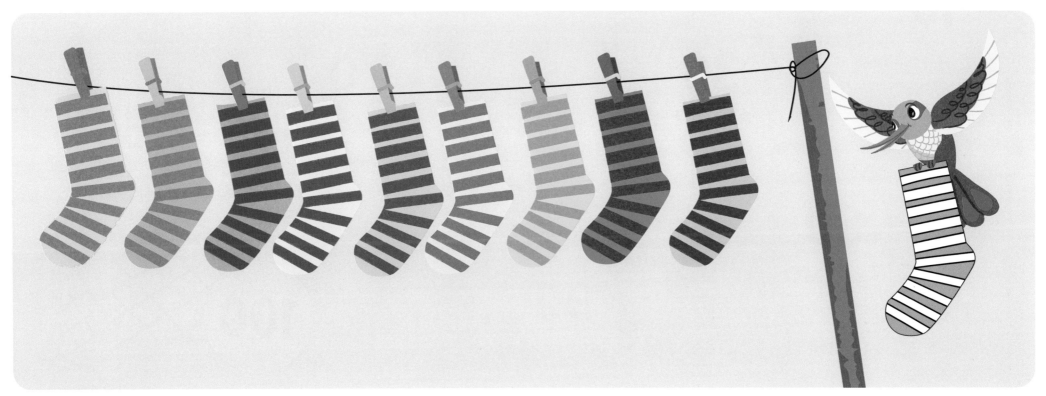

 **Color.**

Chant. **Connect.** **Say.**

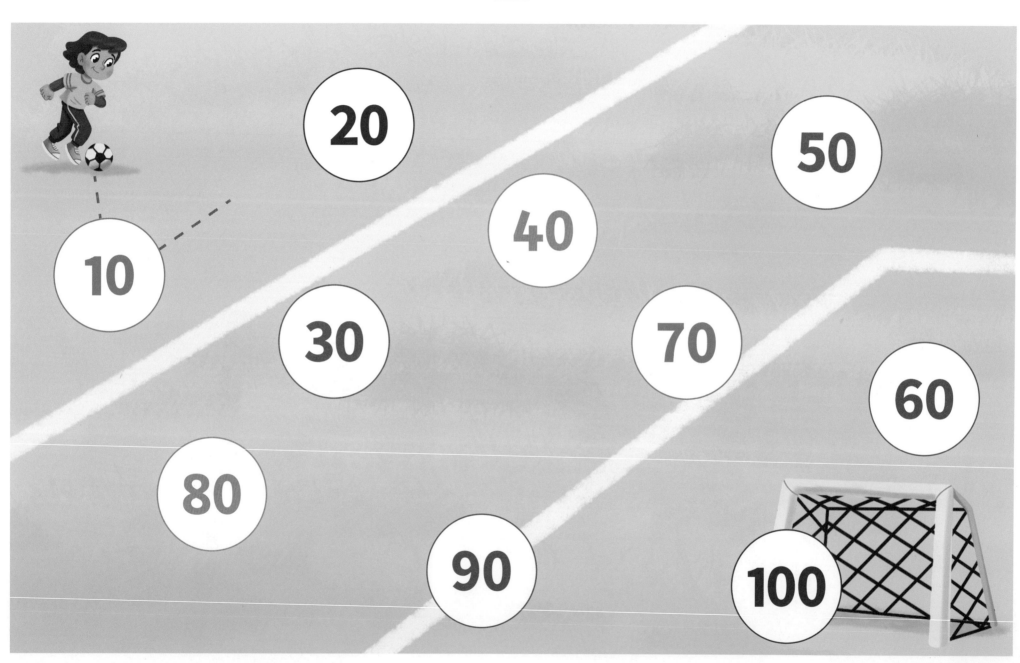

Extra
Color.

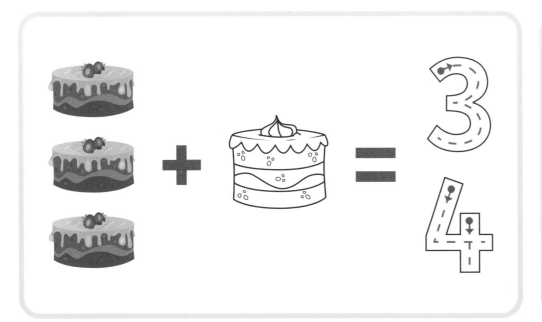

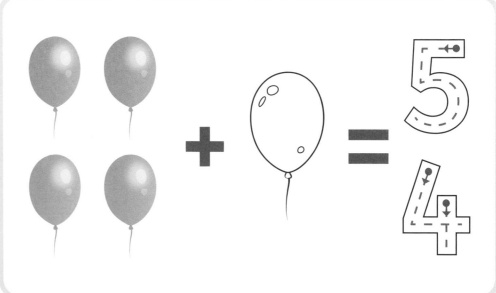

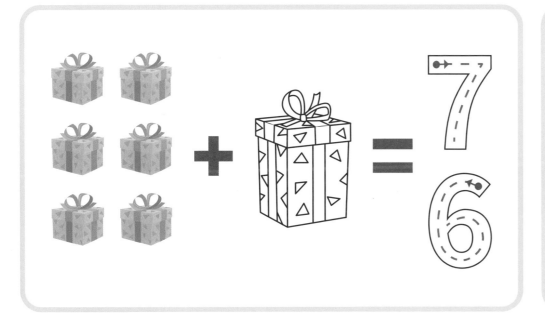

Extra
Color.

₄₃ **Chant.** **Count.** **Trace.**

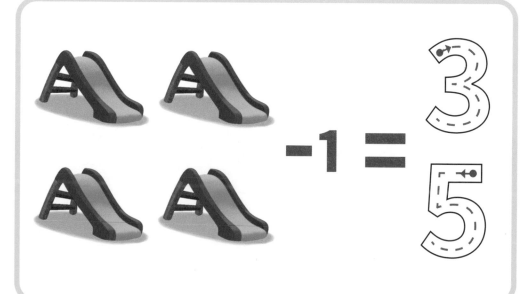

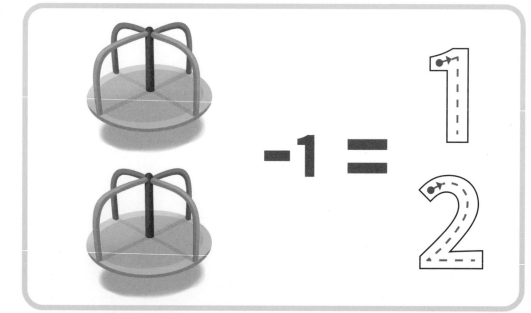

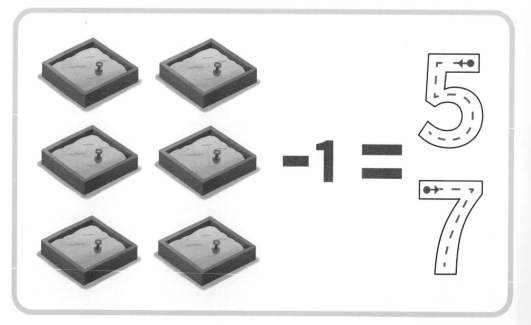

Numbers one less

Extra

Copy.

Stickers

Unit 1 Page 8

Unit 2 Page 16

Stickers

Unit 3 Page 24

Unit 4 Page 32

Stickers

Unit 5 Page 40

Unit 6 Page 48

Stickers

Unit 7 Page 56

Unit 8 Page 64

Unit 9 Page 72

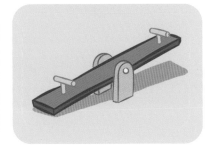